VOLCANOES
AND EARTHQUAKES

Nick Arnold

Wayland

Pirates!

Volcanoes and Earthquakes

Editor: Sarah Doughty
Cover design: Giles Wheeler

Published in 1998 by
Wayland Publishers Ltd
61 Western Road, Hove
East Sussex BN3 1JD

British Library Cataloguing in Publication Data
Arnold, Nick
    Volcano and Earthquake. – (Amazing World)
    1. Natural Disasters – Juvenile literature
    I. Title
    363.3'49

    ISBN 0 7502 2270 0

Printed and bound in Italy by G. Canale & C. S.p.A.

This book is based on *Volcano, Earthquake and Hurricane* by
the same author published in 1996 by Wayland Publishers Ltd.

Picture acknowledgements
Camera Press 5b/N Blickov, 7l, 14-15/Jaccard,
19/Rosenquist/Earth, 23b/ERMA, 25/ERMA, 27b/ERMA,
39b/Vanya Kewley, 42/Anwar Hossain; CM Dixon 4b; Mary
Evans Picture Library 7t, 18b, 39t, 41b; Geoscience Features
4l, 11r, 12t, 12-13, 34; Robert Harding Picture Library 20, 28-
9/Adrian Neville; Hulton Deutsch *cover*, 8 both, 10-11, 17t,
28t, 33t; Image Select 16b, 23l; Impact 22/Paul Forster,
24t/Philip Gordon, 27r/Peter Menzel; Frank Lane Picture
Agency 9t/Tomas Kicek, 21t/USDA, 37t/NASA,
38t/Australian Information Service, 41t/W Carlson; Peter
Newark's Pictures 6, 33b, 35b; Oxford Scientific Films
17c/Dieter and Mary Plage/Survival, 26t/Warren Faidley,
35r/Warren Faidley, 36b/Warren Faidley; Rex Features
13t/SIPA, 14/Carraro, 15t, 31, 40/SIPA/Voja Miladinovic,
cover, 42-3/SIPA/Voja Miladinovic; Science Photo Library 44;
Tony Stone Images 9b/G Brad Lewis, 45/Ken Biggs; Zefa 1,
10b/K Kerth, 30b/Ned Gillette. The artwork is by Peter Bull
16l, 18t, 28b, 30r, 37l, 41c; and Tony Townsend 5t, 7b, 17b,
21b, 24b, 26l, 32, 36t.

Contents

Why is the Earth Restless?

You might think the world is quiet and peaceful. But in some places red-hot rock blasts out of the ground. This is called a volcano and what happens is called a volcanic eruption.

◄ A volcano throws red-hot rocks into the air.

The destruction of Pompeii

In AD 79, a volcano called Vesuvius destroyed the city of Pompeii in Italy. Ash fell on the town, killing 2, 000 people. Romans were buried under ash 18 m deep, which preserved their bodies, homes and belongings for people to see centuries later.

► This dog was buried by ash from Vesuvius.

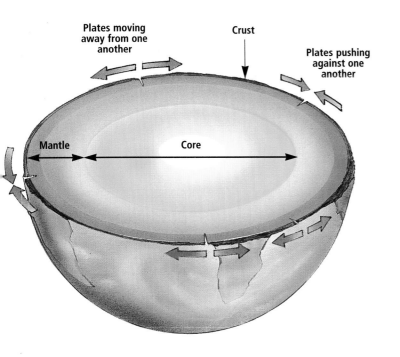

Plates moving away from one another

Crust

Plates pushing against one another

Mantle

Core

◄ The centre of the Earth is very hot. Rock melts deep underground. The solid ground is made up of vast slabs of rock known as plates. These are many kilometres thick and thousands of kilometres across. The plates float on melted rock, called the mantle.

▼ Soldiers work to rescue people after an earthquake in Armenia, in southern Asia, in 1988.

A volcano spits out red-hot rock and smaller lumps of ash. Sometimes the flying ash turns the sky as black as night.

In some parts of the world, the ground under people's feet can suddenly shake like jelly so that houses tumble down. This is called an earthquake.

The air around us is always moving. The winds usually blow gently. But sometimes the winds spin like a top to form a hurricane or a tornado. These winds can blow away a whole town.

What happens when Volcanoes Erupt?

Two thousand years ago, the people of Pompeii, Italy woke up to a bright sunny morning.

Everyone was looking forward to a big parade in the town centre.

◀ The home of a rich person in Pompeii around AD 79. The floor is made from coloured stones forming a picture called a mosaic.

But it never happened. About noon there was an ear-splitting crash. A giant cloud rose from the nearby volcano and soon the sky was filled with ash. Within minutes ash and hot stones were raining down.

In a few days the town was completely buried.

▲ A soldier shelters from the falling ash.

▲ This man's body was covered by ash.

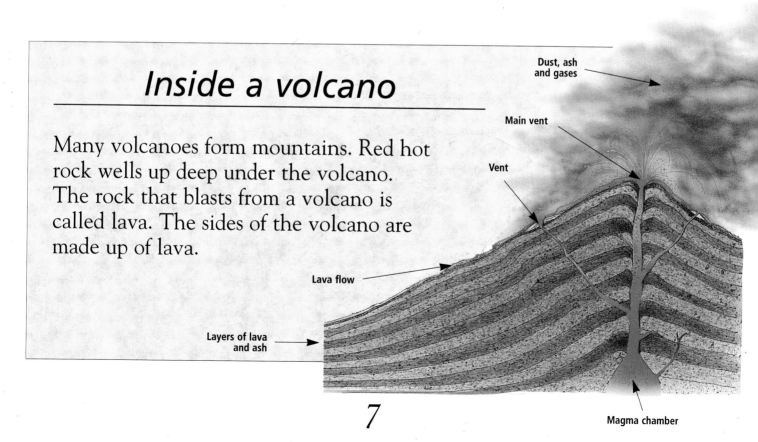

Inside a volcano

Many volcanoes form mountains. Red hot rock wells up deep under the volcano. The rock that blasts from a volcano is called lava. The sides of the volcano are made up of lava.

Dust, ash and gases

Main vent

Vent

Lava flow

Layers of lava and ash

Magma chamber

What happened inside Vesuvius?

Inside the volcano the red-hot lava was under pressure. Then some rocks blocking the opening of the volcano shifted. Red-hot lava blasted out like a fizzy drink squirting from a bottle when the top is taken off.

◄ The last time Vesuvius erupted was in 1944. A huge cloud of gas erupted from the volcano.

Run for your life

A young man named Pliny ran away from a villa outside town with his mother. He later described how the earth shook and how the sky was dark with ash.

Sometimes he could see flames leaping from the volcano. Ash covered the ground like grey snow.

► Pliny and his family watch, with horror, the eruption from their villa.

Frozen in time

Many people had been buried by ash or squashed under falling buildings. Hundreds of years later archaeologists dug up the remains of Pompeii. They found many possessions that belonged to the townsfolk.

◄ Explosions from Stromboli throw rocks high up in the air. Stromboli is a volcanic island in the Mediterranean.

Other types of eruption

Sometimes red-hot lava flows from a volcano. The lava spreads along the ground like boiling treacle.

In other places a volcano blasts red hot rocks into the air like fireworks.

► Red hot lava flows from a volcano in Hawaii in the Pacific Ocean.

9

The end of St Pierre

St Pierre in Martinique was a lovely old town a busy port. But in 1902 Mount Pelée, a nearby volcano, erupted. Ash rained down on the town and piled up in the streets.

▲ St Pierre before the eruption.

The local council told people they were in no danger. But many people were scared and some ran away. Others thought it was safe to stay. But then a terrible thing happened.

◄ St Pierre today. The town is overlooked by the volcano in the background.

The volcano blew up and a sheet of flame rushed towards the town. A rich landowner named Fernand Clerc got away with his wife and children and he described the scene they left behind.

Looking back at St Pierre, Clerc and his family saw fire and a cloud like a black fog. The blast was followed by a terrible fire that burnt the town to ashes.

▲ The remains of St Pierre after the eruption.

▲ The dungeon which protected Sylbaris from the blast.

Few people escaped. In two minutes the whole of St Pierre was wiped out.

In the jail a young man named Louis-Auguste Sylbaris hid in terror. He was never to forget the moment when disaster struck. The thick walls of the prison saved Sylbaris from the blast.

He was rescued three days later, terrified, thirsty and covered in burns.

What happened in St Pierre?

The volcano erupted. Part of the blast rushed down a steep valley towards the town.

It was described by a officer on a ship at sea as being a 'solid wall of flame'. He said the volcano sounded like 'a thousand cannons'.

Mud-slide!

Volcanoes can cause other dangers too. If there is a great deal of rain or snow the lava turns into a torrent of mud. A mud-slide can bury a whole town without trace.

This happened to the town of Armero in Columbia, South America in 1985.

It was a wet night and most people were at home watching television. There was little warning as the mud-slide struck the town. Many families were trapped in their homes.

▲ Armero after the mud-slide. Many houses were buried or swept away.

◄ The volcano continued to erupt. This amazing picture shows another eruption a few months later. The men who took this photograph were lucky to escape alive.

The world is ending!

Sixteen-year-old Slaye Molina was at home with her family when the mud-slide (called a lahar) struck Armero. She says "... At 11.15, the mud came. People screamed "The world is ending!"... We rushed outside."

Some people clamboured on to the roofs of their houses. Others ran to a nearby hill that was higher than the mud. They were stuck there for three miserable days until help arrived.

Rescue work

After a disaster like Armero, doctors and aid workers rush to the area. Their first job is to find people trapped under buildings.

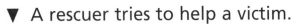

▼ A rescuer tries to help a victim.

Everyone needs food and to find shelter from the cold. Sometimes getting help to people can be difficult and dangerous.

► This baby has been rescued from the mud and wrapped in blankets to keep it warm.

▼ An injured man is taken to hospital.

The Worst Eruptions

Sometimes a volcano does more than destroy a town. A big eruption can wipe out a whole island. This happened to Krakatoa in Indonesia in 1883.

The island was made up of three volcanoes and Krakatoa was the biggest of these. It was a peaceful place and local people made a living by fishing or growing rice.

▲ Krakatoa and its neighbouring islands.

▼ Krakatoa before the eruption. Smoke can be seen rising from the volcano.

▲ The huge cloud of ash from Krakatoa.

One day the two smaller volcanoes began to spit red-hot rock and ash. Within weeks huge blasts shook the ground and made giant waves in the sea. The waves crashed against other islands and swept away many homes.

What happened?

The three volcanoes including part of Krakatoa collapsed into the magma chamber, forming a vast crater.

A new volcano appeared in this crater called 'Anak Krakatoa' or 'child of Krakatoa'.

Since 1927 a new ▲ volcano has grown on the site of Krakatoa.

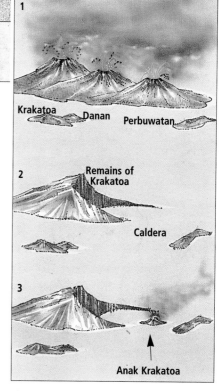

▶ 1. Before the eruption
2. After the eruption
3. Krakatoa today.

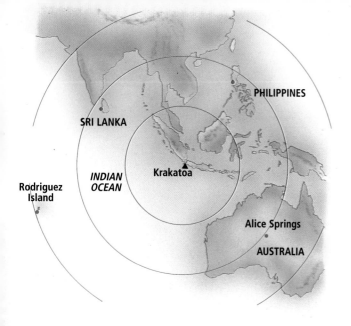

▲ People heard the blast within the area shown on the map.

A big bang

When Krakatoa blew up people heard the roar in far away China and Australia.

The giant waves that were made by the blast were seen on the other side of the world.

Up to 36,000 people died, drowned by the huge wave or killed by disease or hunger after the explosion.

Terror at sea

Passing ships were in terrible danger. Some were hit by the giant waves. The crew of one ship said the sky was black with flying ash. It was so dark they could not even see each other.

► This Dutch warship was swept inland by a giant wave.

Fire Mountain

In 1980 the volcano of Mount St Helens in Washington State, USA, poured out ash. Most of the people living nearby were moved to safety. 84-year old Harry Truman, the owner of the Lodge refused to leave.

It looked as if the volcano was about to blow up. Part of its slope was bulging outwards.

▲ The vast ash cloud of Mount St Helens swallows up a forest.

The blast happened one Sunday morning. A huge mass of rocks and mud poured down the volcano. More ash and rock thundered high into the air.

▲ The forests were devastated and covered with grey ash.

Fortunately, although the blast was so huge few people were killed. Most people had moved to somewhere safer.

◄ The cloud of ash towers above the city of Portland in Oregon.

► The eruption changed the shape of Mt St Helens, blowing the top off the mountain and leaving a crater.

Before

After

But the ash proved a good soil for growing plants.
Today the area is once more covered with trees.

Blasts from the past

There are signs of bigger blasts that happened long ago. Lake Toba in Sumatra covers the site of a volcano that erupted 73,500 years ago. Scientists think the eruption blew out 2,700 times more ash than Mount St Helens.

▼ The peaceful shores of Lake Toba, Sumatra today.

An Earthquake Strikes

An earthquake can be more dangerous than a volcanic eruption. Over 400 years ago a terrible earthquake in China is thought to have killed 830,000 people – many times more than the worst volcanic eruption.

▲ In 1758 a huge earthquake destroyed Lisbon, Portugal.

► This man is escaping from a city hit by an earthquake.

Why earthquakes happen

The surface of the Earth is made up of vast plates. Sometimes two plates grind and stick together. They come unstuck with a mighty shudder that causes an earthquake. The area where this happens is called a fault. Most people live well away from faults and their homes are safe from earthquakes.

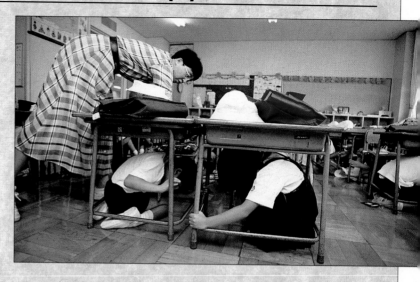

▲ Japanese children are taught to shelter from an earthquake.

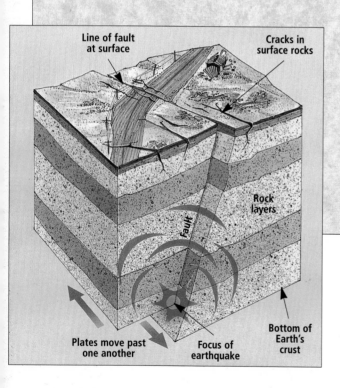

Line of fault at surface

Cracks in surface rocks

Rock layers

Fault

Plates move past one another

Focus of earthquake

Bottom of Earth's crust

◄ Plates move and cause an earthquake. Shock waves spread out from the focus at a speed of several km/sec.

Earthquakes today

Earthquakes can still cause dreadful damage even in a modern city. In 1989 an earthquake hit the city of San Francisco and wrecked thousands of buildings. The earthquake struck late one afternoon.

▼ Cars piled up after the earthquake.

Measuring earthquakes

Scientists measure the shaking of an earthquake using a machine called a seismometer. The shocks cause a pen to make zig-zag marks. Tall zig-zags mean a more powerful earthquake.

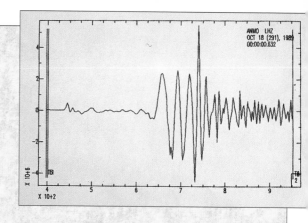

▲ The seismograph of the 1989 San Francisco earthquake.

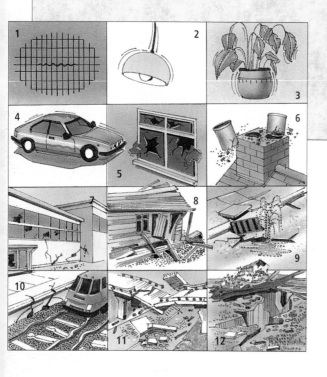

◄ The scale of 1-12 for measuring the power of an earthquake.

When the San Francisco earthquake struck, people were going about their daily business, and many were driving home from work.

Thousands of other people were at a baseball game. Suddenly the whole stadium started to shake. A huge gap opened up in the seating.

Everyone was scared and as the stadium shook, all the players ran on to the pitch hoping to be out of the way of falling stands. Many of the spectators were terrified. Luckily no-one was hurt.

But elsewhere in the city huge fires were raging, bridges collapsed and roads opened wide.

◄ These people are happy to find each other still alive.

► The earthquake wrecked many roads in the city.

▲ The remains of San Francisco after an earthquake in 1906.

What happened

Earthquakes occur along deep cracks called faults. The plates that make up the nearby San Andreas fault suddenly shifted. The shock caused the earthquakes.

In 1906 the same fault caused a terrible earthquake that also wrecked San Francisco.

Map labels:

USA

Sacramento

San Francisco

Las Vegas

San Andreas Fault

Santa Barbara

Los Angeles

PACIFIC OCEAN

San Diego

MEXICO

▲ The map shows the San Andreas Fault in California, USA.

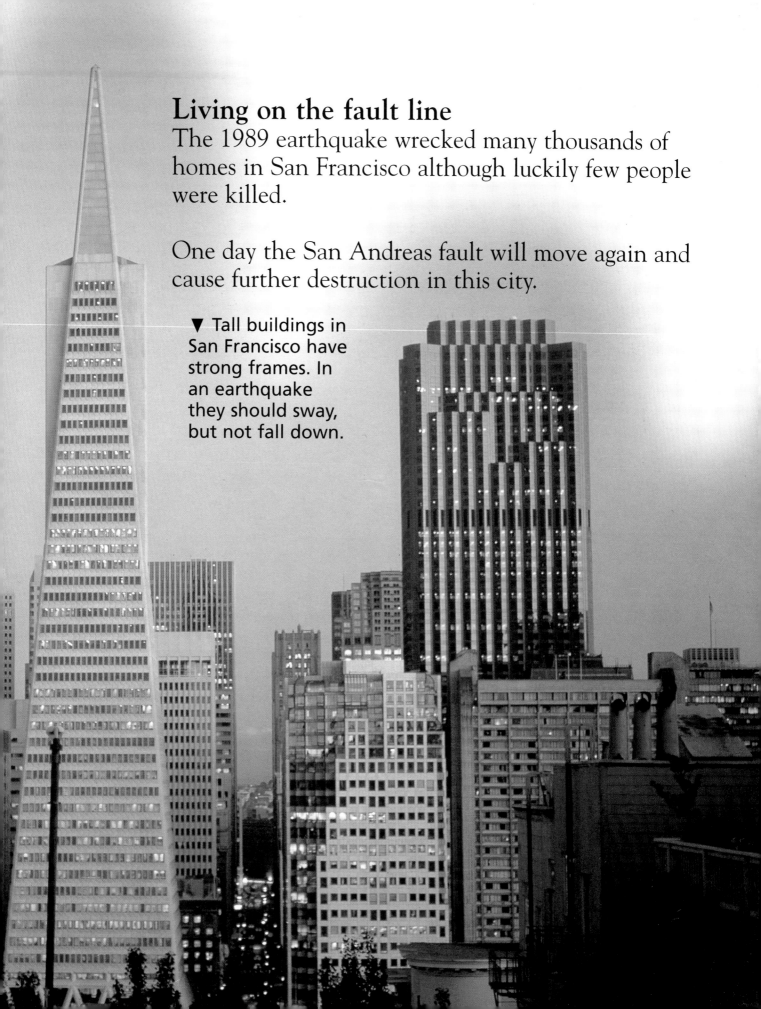

Living on the fault line

The 1989 earthquake wrecked many thousands of homes in San Francisco although luckily few people were killed.

One day the San Andreas fault will move again and cause further destruction in this city.

▼ Tall buildings in San Francisco have strong frames. In an earthquake they should sway, but not fall down.

Other Disasters caused by Earthquakes

Sometimes an earthquake does more than simply shake the ground. It can knock masses of rock and mud down a hillside. Anything in the way of this thundering mass is swept away or crushed.

PERU
BRAZIL
ANDES MOUNTAINS
Yungay
BOLIVIA
Lima
PACIFIC
OCEAN
La Paz

This was the fate of Yungay in Peru in 1970. The disaster happened one afternoon at the end of May. Most of the people were indoors watching football on television. They felt the ground shaking. It was a powerful earthquake.

◄ An avalanche happens when a mass of snow and ice slips down a mountain.

They rushed outside to see a huge mass of rock rushing towards their town. It all happened so quickly that few people had a chance to get away. Within minutes the beautiful town of Yungay had been flattened by tumbling rocks.

◄ The area of Yungay and the Andes mountains in Peru.

► These children escaped the disaster. They are dressed warmly to keep out the cold.

Lucky to be alive

Some people in Yungay ran to a nearby hill. Senor Casaverde, a survivor, reported "I reached the upper part of the hill just in time, as the debris avalanche hit the lower slopes." The hill was higher than the wave of rocks. The people were safe there. Some of them reached the hill with only seconds to spare.

▶ The sea bed drops causing the giant wave or tsunami.

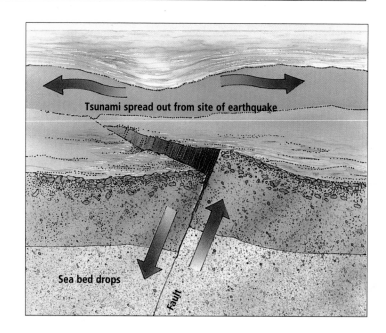

Terrible tsunami

An earthquake under the sea can make a huge wave called a tsunami. One August day in 1868 a tsunami swept ashore at the town of Arica, Chile. But before this the town was rocked by a huge earthquake. Many buildings fell down.

A US ship the *Wateree* was in the bay at the time. The crew saw the sea rushing in and out as the earthquake struck. A few hours later a look-out on *Wateree* spotted a giant wave. The tsunami had arrived. There was no escape.

▲ A tsunami can easily wreck a big ship.

▼ This ship has been washed up a hill by a tsunami which struck in 1964.

With a crash the wave hit *Wateree* and plunged her under the water. As the ship came to the surface the huge wave swept her three km inland. The crew were lucky to be alive.

▼ A tsunami hits the island of Hawaii. The man arrowed is in deadly danger.

What happened

During an undersea earthquake the sea bed moves suddenly. The sea move forwards and then backwards, causing a tsunami. The tsunami gets higher as it nears the shore.

A Hurricane Strikes

Imagine a terrible storm with winds strong enough to blow down houses and carry away trees. This is a hurricane.

These huge storms can be over 2,000 km wide. The wind swirls around a calm area called the eye. A hurricane can wreck a town just like a powerful earthquake.

▲ A hurricane hits the coast of Florida, USA.

◄ A helicopter rescue. A house has been wrecked by a hurricane.

What causes hurricanes?

Hurricanes form when warm air rises off the sea. The Earth is spinning in space. As the Earth turns the warm air also spins round. More air is sucked inwards as the hurricane gets bigger and bigger.

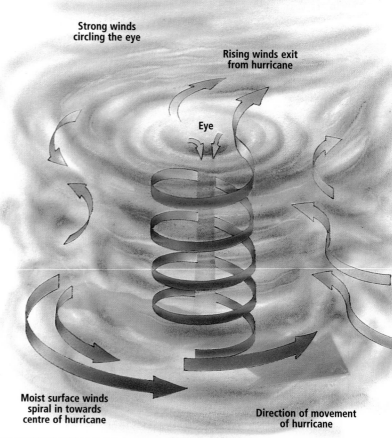

Strong winds circling the eye

Rising winds exit from hurricane

Eye

Moist surface winds spiral in towards centre of hurricane

Direction of movement of hurricane

▲ Air spins inwards into the hurricane.

◄ A closer view of the damage caused by the hurricane in Florida, USA.

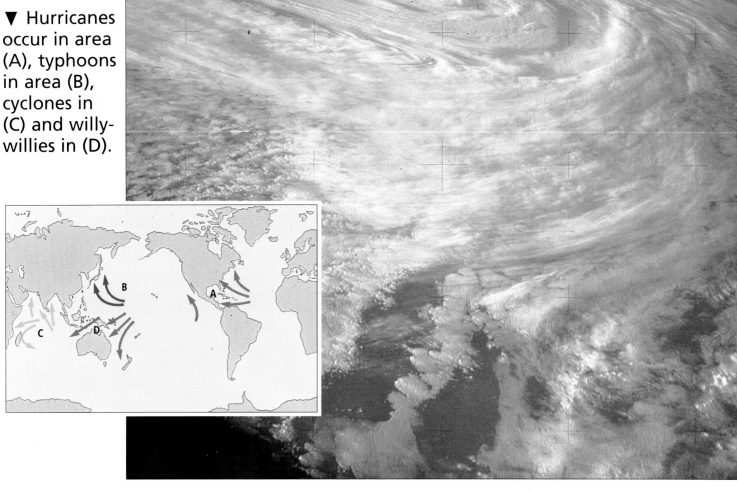

► A hurricane seen from space.

▼ Hurricanes occur in area (A), typhoons in area (B), cyclones in (C) and willy-willies in (D).

In different parts of the world hurricanes are called cyclones, typhoons or willy-willies. To tell them apart each storm is given a name. The first storm of the year has a name starting with 'A'. The second storm begins with 'B' and so on.

◄ Darwin after Cyclone Tracy. This house has been torn to pieces by the wind.

Cyclone Tracy

On Christmas Day, 1974, the city of Darwin, Australia was smashed to pieces by Cyclone Tracy. Most people were at home. Children were opening their presents and grown-ups were snoozing after a lovely Christmas dinner.

The wind grew stronger and stronger. Buildings began to blow down and cars were rolled about like toys. People sheltered under beds as the wind wrecked their homes. The cyclone was so violent that nine-tenths of the city was destroyed.

Afterwards, many families cooked food outside because they had no kitchens. People set up groups to care for the injured until help arrived.

The hurricane that hit Darwin in 1974 caused a great deal of damage, but few people lost their lives.

On 30 April 1991, a cyclone hit the densely-populated area of Bangladesh, where the loss of life was much worse.

Danger in Bangladesh

Thousands of people live on islands off the coast of Bangladesh. But these islands are very flat. They are in danger from floods caused by cyclones.

▲ This cyclone is wrecking the houseboat of a Chinese family in Hong Kong in 1906.

◄ The low-lying islands of Bangladesh are easily flooded by the sea.

▲ A Bangladeshi village wrecked by the cyclone in 1991. The dead animals were drowned in floods.

The people of the islands live in huts that are easily blown away by strong winds. Although life is dangerous the people stay because the soil is good for growing crops.

Danger – Tornado!

A tornado is a spinning storm that takes shape inside a thundercloud. Unlike a hurricane, a tornado appears over dry land. Most tornadoes happen in central USA and Australia.

▲ A tornado in the USA.

Tornadoes are smaller than hurricanes – they are not more than a few hundred metres across. But as the tornado sucks in more air it gets bigger and stronger. Soon it can blow away buildings.

▲ The area of the USA where tornadoes are common.

► A tornado in Australia in 1939. A tornado moves at 120 km/hr – much faster than the people can run.

▲ The cyclone caused terrible floods. These people are rescuing their belongings.

The islanders listened to the radio for news of the storm. Meanwhile the wind grew stronger. Soon houses began to blow down. As the eye of the cyclone passed overhead the waves rose higher and higher.

Huge waves washed away what was left of the houses. Thousands of people died and those who escaped had to cling to trees or wreckage.

▼ A boy and his father who survived the 1991 cyclone in Bangladesh, in front of their wrecked home.

Hurricanes, earthquakes and volcanoes are so powerful that we cannot stop them happening. All we can do is to find out where they will strike and when.

Then we can warn people so they can get away to a safe place.

▼ A hurricane seen from space with added colours to show windy areas. The red areas show where the winds are strongest.

► A hurricane blows huge waves ashore.

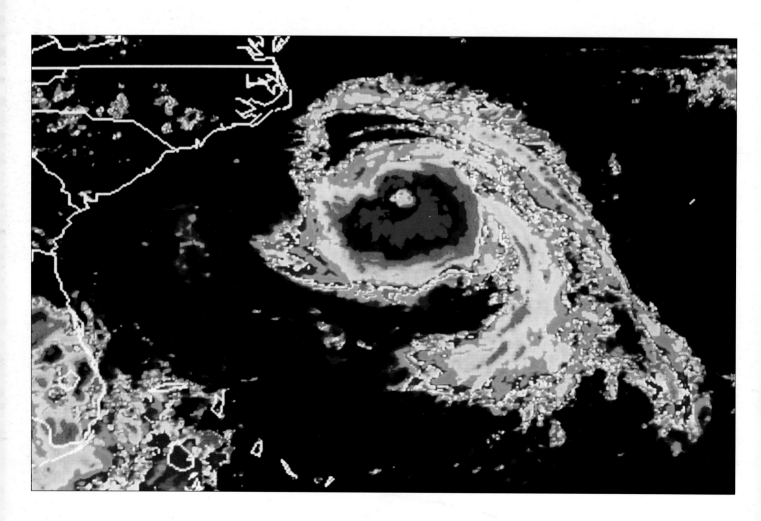

The storm surge

The waves became higher as the eye of a cyclone arrives. This is because the winds press down on the sea. But in the eye the water bulges upwards. As this raised-up water hits the shore huge waves swept over the land. Storm surges have often hit the islands of Bangladesh.

Timeline

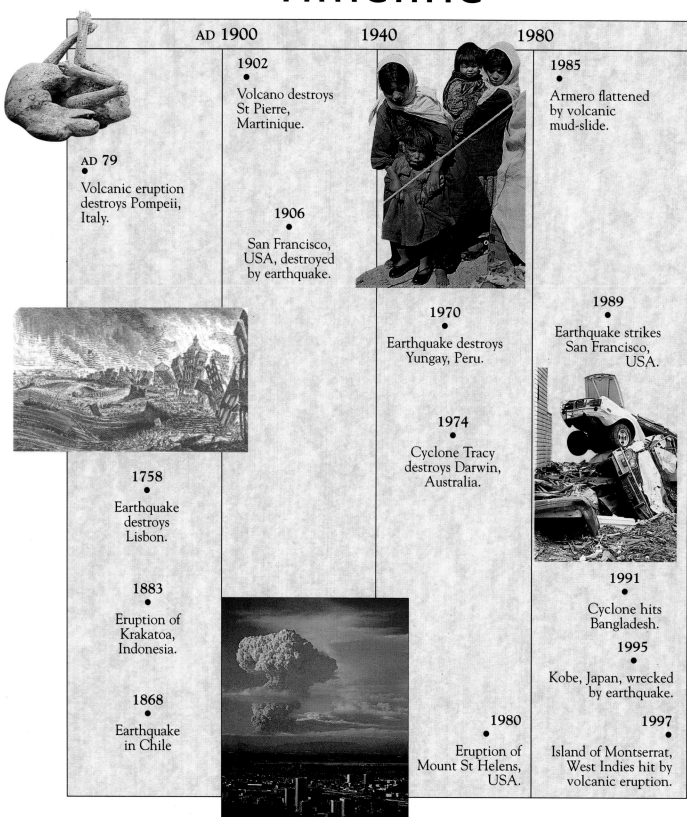

AD 1900   1940   1980

AD 79
Volcanic eruption destroys Pompeii, Italy.

1758
Earthquake destroys Lisbon.

1883
Eruption of Krakatoa, Indonesia.

1868
Earthquake in Chile

1902
Volcano destroys St Pierre, Martinique.

1906
San Francisco, USA, destroyed by earthquake.

1970
Earthquake destroys Yungay, Peru.

1974
Cyclone Tracy destroys Darwin, Australia.

1980
Eruption of Mount St Helens, USA.

1985
Armero flattened by volcanic mud-slide.

1989
Earthquake strikes San Francisco, USA.

1991
Cyclone hits Bangladesh.

1995
Kobe, Japan, wrecked by earthquake.

1997
Island of Montserrat, West Indies hit by volcanic eruption.

Glossary

Archaeologist Someone who digs up old buildings to find out how people lived.

Ash Small bits of rock blasted from a volcano.

Core The centre of the Earth.

Fault A line where two plates meet and grind together.

Lava A type of molten rock that erupts from volcanoes.

Mantle A part of the Earth made up of the solid and molten rock.

Plates Huge slabs of rock that make up the Earth's surface and are often thousands of kilometres across.

Pressure When things are pressed together very tightly.

Surface The outside part of an object.

Tsunami A giant wave caused by an undersea earthquake.

Further Information

Information books:

Closer Look at Earthquakes by Joyce Pope (Franklin Watts, 1996)

Closer Look at Hurricanes and Typhoons by Jen Green (Franklin Watts, 1996)

Closer Look at Volcanoes by Jen Green (Franklin Watts, 1996)

Flood Damage by Susan Bullen (Wayland, 1994)

Volcanoes by Neil Morris (Crabtree Publishing, 1996)

Index